The Luton Hat Trade
A Brief History
By
Alex Askaroff

The rights of Alex Askaroff as author
of this work have been asserted by him
in accordance with the Copyright,
Designs and Patents Act 1993.
©

To see other publications by
Alex Askaroff visit Amazon

This is no masterpiece. It's more a self-published labour of love from someone who has spent a lifetime in the sewing trade and a million hours gathering facts for you. From my vast profits of around sixpence a book I'll invest in some sweet peas to make my allotment sparkle with colour. Why write it? Well no one else bothers! Please forgive my spelling, United Kingdom English, and enjoy it in the same spirit that it was written.

Many thanks to Mandy Finch for the final read through.

The Luton Hat Trade
A Brief History
By
Alex Askaroff

The Luton Hat trade

Almost every person at some time in their lives has worn a hat. However there was a time when leaving the house without one was almost a crime.

The hat industry reached a peak just before the outbreak of The Great War in Britain. Statistics show that in 1911 around 30,000,000 hats were produced in a single year. Hardly a head was seen outdoors not supporting some kind of hat!

There was a period when it seemed like every self-respecting family would have a row of hat pegs in the hall or behind the front door and not be seen out without some sort of head apparel.

Hats were also status symbols and a strict class system emerged based on what you plonked on your bonce!

Tradesman would wear different hats to factory workers. The factory foreman wore another style as did the bank manager with his brushed black bowler. Then there was the company boss with his silk lined top of the line beaver trimmed special, the latest fashion model, or the classy retro classic. The gamekeeper would touch the brim of his peeked cap to the lord of the manor with his Regency Topper. Then the military caught on adding a whole new raft of headwear to its ranks.

All of these had to be made by specialists in the hat trade. The hat trade flourished all over England but none compared to Luton which became the centre for hat production on an enormous scale.

Astonishingly at Luton's height the town was producing around 7,000,000 hats a year! Every person wore and owned several hats for different conditions and occasions.

It was also one of the most common presents to receive for birthday or Christmas. In its height in the 19th Century almost every person in Luton was in some way connected to the hat trade.

K. R. Snoxell & Sons Ltd
24-26 Clarendon Road
Luton 24704

The Civic Boater and plaited ladies summer straw hat

Today as I write there are only a handful of hat businesses left in Luton and all are small scale. However exciting things are happening...

Come with me on a journey through one of our great industries of Old England.

Chapter One
As Mad As A Hatter

Let me first explain where the phrase that many of us still use today, 'as mad as a hatter', came from. No it didn't come from Alice's adventures in Wonderland.

From around the 1850's a new process called "carroting" was used in the making of felt hats. The animal skins (especially rabbit) were rinsed in a carrot coloured solution of the mercury compound, and mercury nitrate. It helped to help remove the fur from the pelt leaving the fine felt to be used for hat making.

No one clearly understood at the time the deadly consequences of these operations on the workers.

This process separated the fur from the pelt and matted it together. The vapours did not seem too bad (even though some of the methods also included human urine).

But the vapours produced were actually highly toxic, leading to a lot of mercury poisoning in the hat industry.

The psychological symptoms associated with mercury poisoning led to workers behaving erratically in an almost insane manner. It was this behaviour so commonplace in the hat industry which inspired the phrase 'as mad as a hatter.' There were many other side effects as well, including shaking muscles and spasms.

The use of mercury in the felt and hat industry was banned in 1941 after autopsy's on hatters found holes in their brain tissue the size of marbles!

However it gets worse for the poor hatter. If the mercury didn't get you then the alcohol did.

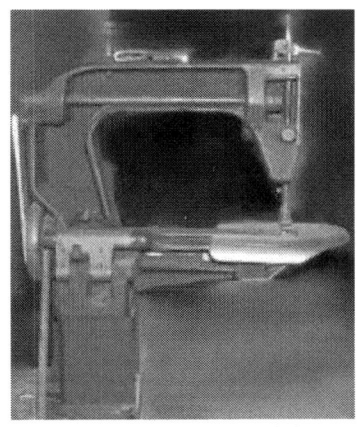

Notice how hat machines traditionally sits well above the workbench to allow access to the hat, sewn in a circular motion around the machine bed.

Chapter Two
Penny Lane

The other big killer of the poor workforce was alcohol. Many hatters also died of Cirrhosis of the liver. Why?

In the hat trade Uric acid from urine was used to soften (and sometimes harden) the pelts. It had been used historically all over the world to treat animal skins.

Unbelievably, as demanded peeked, urine was becoming expensive to buy! Households often saved their buckets of urine to sell. They were sold for a penny a bucket to the urine collector (hence the term taking the piss). I hope you're smiling now! The collector picked up daily at the end of many city streets.

The densely populated inner cities, where thousands of people lived in terraced rows, was the ideal source of this much needed product. It is the reason why so many built up city areas still have a street called Penny Lane.

The hat makers came up with their own cunning plan to save money. Hat factories got around some of this expense by brewing huge amounts of beer for their workers.

The hatters and staff were encouraged to drink as much as they liked all day, as long as it did not affect their work. All the urine was collected and the uric acid was used in the manufacturing process to cure the pelts or skins.

This huge amount of alcohol, drunk on a daily basis, led many a poor hatter to die of liver failure before the mercury got them! In the 'good old days' before health & safety, if the madness didn't get you the booze did!

Let's not concentrate on the down side here but the wonderful hat industry that, since science has proven and removed most of the deadly chemicals in the industry, has cleaned up its act.

Today, the hat trade in Luton is only a tiny part of a huge worldwide industry. Like I say everyone use to wear hats, especially the men. Even in my youth it was rare to see a bare head. I remember seeing pictures of London in the 1930's where thousands of people were rushing here-there-and-everywhere and nearly every head had a hat on it. Luton was producing millions hats a year at the time! Certainly no self-respecting person would possibly leave home without cover.

Hat making was big business and Luton in England was at its centre. There were other hat makers around the country and there was a large hat industry in Stockport, Manchester which at its height was producing around 6 million hats a year! There is currently a great museum there dedicated to the old industry.

Almost any town could hold a hatter or milliner. Many times the smaller businesses went hand in hand with what the locals wanted, like coats and dresses, suits and gloves. General outfitters became a common sight in most towns.

By the late Victorian period the straw boater became a popular summer hat. Notice the endless circles of straw stitched around and around. Hats could also be braided or plaited without stitching.

Here I am with an Anita B straw machine made by the German firm of Guhl & Harbeck circa 1890. Heinrich Grossman also made a similar machine in Dresden. These small machines ran for decades in businesses and would stitch at over 3,800 stitches per minute without a problem. Notice the special alloy stand to allow access for the hats. I seem to have been fixing machines for the hat industry most of my life.

Chapter Three
The New Failsworth Hat Manufacturing Company

One of the survivors and most successful hat makers outside of Luton is Failsworth Hats Limited of Manchester. Amazingly they are still in business today.

Beginning at the Maypole Hat Works, the firm started as a cottage industry in 1875. As the business grew they became the Failsworth Hat Manufacturing Company. They began building an envious reputation for quality. Initially less than 30 handmade hats were produced a week, mainly for their local market, but as their fame grew, so did the order books.

In 1881, with the need for larger premises, the production of hat manufacture moved to Claremont Street in Failsworth. By 1903 the business had become renowned for their silk hats, with 300 hats a week now being made. In the same year the 'New Failsworth Hat Manufacturing Company' became incorporated. 1903 is the date that they became firmly established.

Denton, a district of Manchester that concentrated on hats, made over 24,000 felted hats per week!

In 1920's Eastbourne, George Brown & Co in Terminus Road supplied Failsworth hats to their customers.

The company boomed as hats reached a peak in 1914. By the outbreak of WW2 the company was producing an astonishing quarter of a million hats a month. In 1940 the name of the company changed to Failsworth Hats Limited.

The company carried on adapting with the ever changing market and new trends. During the following years they started replacing the old traditional skins and furs with high fashion designs.

In 1998, to make way for the re-development of the new Failsworth Centre, the business moved just around the corner to 13 Crown Street.

The company is still booming with modern fashion fabrics in over 150 styles and 1,350 colour combinations.

Failsworth Hats Limited is one of the few great success stories in the British hat industry, learning from the ever changing market and adapting to consumer demand. The business carries over 100,000 hats in stock at any one time.

Harris Tweed & Cord Flat Caps

Flat caps have been making a big comeback in recent years. Traditional fabrics like Harris Tweed have found great new markets, appealing to all ages and levels of society, from the gamekeeper to the football star.

Chapter Four
Ladies of the Night. I beg your pardon—Hat Makers!

The hat trade was one of the few industries where women workers flourished. In 1913 a 'plaiter' who wove the straw into various shapes could earn between 12 to 16 shillings a week, vastly more than say a housemaid or servant.

This led to the woman of the house often earning more than the husband, something unheard of in Britain. It was the first recorded time of the 'house husband'. This caused concern amongst the religious houses as some men apparently turned to drink and 'wastrel ways'. For the women it was hard but rewarding work, allowing them to have a disposable income. Unheard of in austere rural areas.

Many plaiters were mistaken for prostitutes as they dressed in far finer clothes than their other female counterparts. It was wrongly assumed their income could have only come from such a profession!

John Banbury, London House, Woodstock, Oxford. Over 1,000 patterns to choose from!

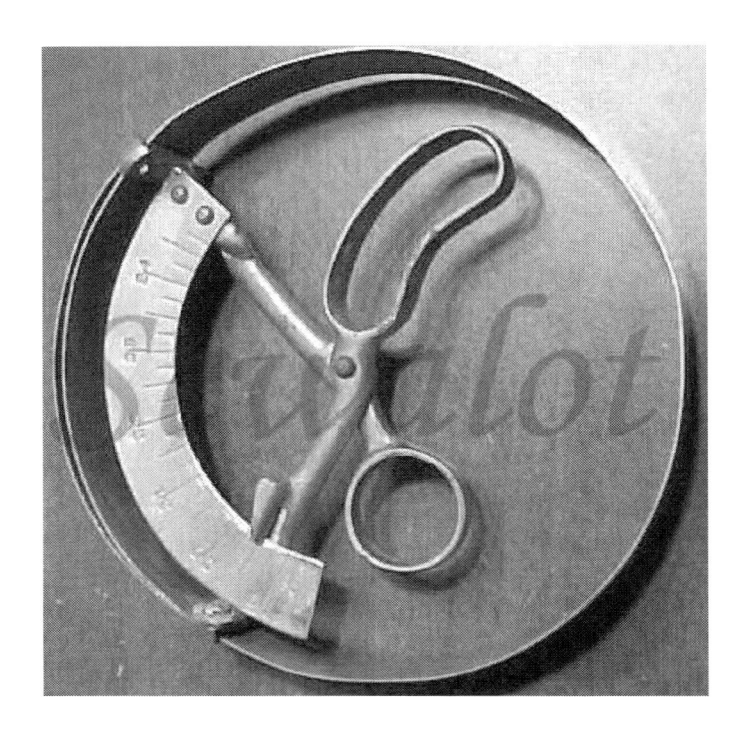

A measure for measuring the internal hat size to match to a new hat. If you had a favourite hat that had become the perfect shape and size of your head, this was the ideal tool. Milliners and hatters all had these specialised instruments.

Chapter Five
When Did It All Start In Luton?

The hat making industry in Luton may have started as early as the turn of the 17th century as in 1610 the quality of the straw and reeds in the outlying areas of Luton were being mentioned in London publications.

No one is EXACTLY sure why the hat industry blossomed in Luton, just north of London, at such an early date. We do know that over the next 400 years hats became synonymous with the town.

There are a few fanciful tales and legends but precious few facts. One legend tells that Mary Queen of Scots son, James, brought the hat trade with him when he claimed the crown of England in 1603 after our first Queen Elizabeth's demise. James was a dandy for a fine hat and apparently had his own team of hat makers.

It is a far-fetched thought but with its abundance of cheap skilled farm labour, materials, and proximity to the Capital, there were many reasons for Luton to become one of the main centres of the hat making in England.

The rich grain fields that surrounded Luton provided perfect material as did the reeds from the low lying marsh areas. Originally a Saxon settlement or 'Tun' on the side of the River Lea, as it grew into a bustling town it became known as Lea-Tun and eventually Luton.

Illustrated London News
1884

This stunning image from The Illustrated London News shows a Plaiter in action with a sheaf of wheat straw under her arm plaiting or weaving it into a braid ready for hat making.

On the farms at harvest time the reapers would reap the grain (usually wheat around Luton) with a sickle or scythe. The straw would be bound into sheaves and supplied to the plaiters. They would clean, sort and size the straw, dyeing it if needed. The plaiters would then split, flatten and shape the straw. At this point the straw could be fashioned into anything from a corn dolly to a stool seat. In the case of hat making they would braid the straw ready for the hat makers. It was often referred to as 'wheat weaving'. This woven strip is what the hat makers would buy to make into their straw hats.

The plaiting and hat industry blossomed and census shows that thousands of straw plaiters and dyers were employed in the area as Luton boomed into an industrial powerhouse of manufacturing. Plaiters became so essential to life around the town that it was taught to children at home and in school.

The industry boomed and records show that by the 1680's thousands of people in the Luton area were being employed making hats. Remember this was long before the Industrial Revolution so nearly all of hat production was labour intensive.

The town also did well during the Napoleonic Wars when an embargo was enforced by Napoleon's Fleet, stifling trade with Europe and the world. Straw for Luton hats did not have to be imported, so supplies continued untouched. However straw plaits imported from Europe were blocked. Luton quickly picked up other towns orders and thrived.

While imports of fur skins, especially beaver's skins from Canada, that were so popular for hats in the

19th Century, were stifled. Luton carried on. Strangely this blockade by Napoleon probably saved the Canadian Beaver from extinction as it was being mercilessly hunted for its waterproof fine fur pelt. Silk hats eventually superseded beaver as the choice of the wealthy when choosing a new hat.

However while the Napoleonic Wars may have saved the Canadian Beaver it saw a slow decline for men's flamboyant high fashion. Men's hats had evolved to match their female counterparts and had been as bright and fashionable as women's. However after the French Revolution in 1789 plainer colours, dress, and sober headwear became commonplace.

Even after the Napoleonic Wars heavy taxes on straw imports kept Luton safe from recession.

Although hat fashion changed, the wearing of hats carried on at a pace. Records show that the height of the Luton Hat Trade was the late 19th century, when almost every family in Luton had a connection with the hat industry.

Of course in that period almost every person from a beggar to a baron wore a hat, right down to the news boys, who in Birmingham wore the notorious flat caps with razor blades sewn into their peaks! Peaky Blinders, as they became known, were apparently lawless gangs of ruthless kids. Their caps were based on a cross between the eight panel Irish farmer's cap and the Scots Bonnet of the 14th Century, similar to a Shelby or golf cap today.

The most likely reason Luton flourished as a centre for hat production was simply raw materials and the difficulty in travel in olden days. Historians have shown that when expertise in a field was learnt and travel was so difficult, the expertise often stayed in the same area, much like the Cycle industry in Coventry or the Needle industry in Redditch. Hatton Gardens is still a diamond centre. Brick Lane in London (where some of my French Huguenot family came to in 1685), is still one of the best places to buy silk (over three centuries after the first silk-traders moved there). From Sheffield Steel to Nottingham Lace, trades often stayed put.

Today, moving of equipment and people is so easy that these special industries are now spread over the whole world. Interestingly many of the remaining hat businesses in Luton don't even make hats, they just import ready-made hats from around the globe. Raffia or palm leaf makes a pretty good substitute for Luton wheat.

A trade in Luton that once boasted over 100,000 workers is now down to a handful of specialists.

However some hats are still produced in the town today, like Walter Wright of Luton, though on a much diminished scale.

What is the difference between a hatter and a milliner?

Although today the lines are blurred there has long been an established and subtle difference between a hatter and a milliner. A hatter is traditionally some person, individual or establishment that sells mainly men's hats and a milliner is the same that sells female hats.

The super rare Singer 103W3. Worth a mint today. They were often belt driven from steam engines housed in a building nearby.

So now let us travel forward in time to the 1960's where we have real tales from real workers in the final days of the booming Luton hat trade.

Chapter Six
Luton Tales

Linda Kilpatrick was a hat maker towards the end of Luton's domination of the hat trade in the 1960's.

In her own words you can travel back with her to the Luton Hat Trade as it really was.

The Hat Trade in Luton 1962-1965 By Linda Kilpatrick- nee Greenwood. Here is her story.

In June 1962 I turned fifteen years old and two weeks later my school life ended. Leaving school at fifteen was quite normal at that time in British history as only the most fortunate stayed on at school until aged sixteen and went on for further education studies.

I was the fourth down of eight children and it was my turn to get a job and contribute to the family income.

There were tons of hat factories in Luton in the 1960's but most are gone now. My sister worked in the hat trade before her marriage and then for seven years did the trimming from home when her son was small. This outwork flourished around the town.

I left home the Monday morning after my school life ended and walked along the back roads of

Luton, Bedfordshire and stopped at every hat factory along Guildford Street.

Guildford Street has since been ripped down for big car parks and buildings as Luton is now a University town and everything has changed.

Chance or fate took me through the doors of a company named J. Collett who had premises in Luton and a showroom in London. I have no clue if it was a family business and it's as if every trace of them has since disappeared.

After I applied at the office I was taken up to the third floor where many odd looking sewing machines filled a room with mostly ladies and girls working on them. Small frosted paned windows lined one wall which was at the front of the building.

I was told to sit down in front of a flatbed machine and was handed a piece of woollen felt. I was then told to sew in circles, which I later found out was my 'aptitude test'. I obviously passed the test as I was then passed to a man (the foreman of that section) at the end of a line of odd looking machines and was given a vacant machine next to him to start my training.

The machine I began my training on was similar to the Wilcox and Gibbs and I started learning how to put Petersham (Grosgrain in America) sizing bands inside ladies woollen felt hats. While doing this I also added the firm's label to each hat.

Although the machine worked in chain stitch and a mistake was easily unravelled, I was told it was important not to make continuous mistakes as the needle marks would compromise the hat. Although it was summer time, all the work done during that time was on winter hats ready for the new season.

In winter we switched to summer hats. On the machine shop floor there were several foremen or forelady's and each section had someone in command.

I was moved around the entire floor during my four years working at this factory and was also used as a 'runner' to run various errands on other floors.

All work was paid by the piece and with piece-work you have to be quick to earn a living. Some girls were slow and some fast.

The Hat Factory consisted of four floors in total and each floor was set up specifically for every part of the hat making process. The hat making started from the top floor where it was set up for blocking and cutting.

I will always remember the pleasant family men who worked up there embroiled in constant hot steam and the smells of wet woollen felt. They always greeted me with smiles and answered any questions I had from my foreman or handed me what I had been sent up there to get.

I then understood why steam blocking was done on the top floor (by the blockers) as constant steam made all walls and ceilings soaking wet. After blocking was finished, the cutting and trimming of the extra felt around the brim edges was also done on this floor.

The men were surrounded by piled up woollen felted hat mounds around their cutting machines and the floor all around them was coated with circle strips of woollen felt. I'm sure they stopped at times to clear a path. I would run the back stairs from the machine floor up to this floor many times during any day as the elevator was always full of large carts on wheels full of hats in various stages.

The next floor down was the sewing machining floor and there were always carts full of hats waiting in line to be delivered to each machine section.

Paper tickets hung off the sides of the carts with specific orders and instructions. Each of us would go to a cart in line and pick up a stack of hats and return to our machine and put the sizing bands in, or other jobs entailed in this stage.

In summer I worked in the 'box' machine section, where a line of sewing machines that looked like box shapes were set up around long industrial tables where they were bolted down. Bundles of coloured straw, sat in the large push carts and we were handed notes which were our orders.

I am happy to say that I was extremely good at the job of making straw hats very quickly, which didn't always win me good points from my co-workers but gave me a reasonable wage.

A wood block in the shape of a crown and brim sat at my left side and I would start with whatever coloured straw I had orders for. These blocks came in various head sizes. I threaded the start of a bundle of straw into the threader of the machine, curved the start of the hat straw into tiny neat circle and then began chain stitching while working the straw into the shape of the block.

When the crown looked close to the size of the block I removed it from the machine to check my sizing. Fortunately I had a great aptitude for guessing size and was rarely wrong. This was important as straw plaiting could not be undone and redone without damage.

Once I knew it was right, I placed it back on the machine until the brim looked complete, then tried it on the block again. Then a quick last finish on the machine to curve the final edge, to round out the brim. I then placed it on the stack of finished hats beside me. When my orders were complete I restacked them into another cart. Some of the blocks were heated and you had to have iron fingers when working with them.

When hats left our floor they made it down to the second floor, which had been set up for trimming and packing. I often ran down to this floor to either pick up or take a hat back to the machine floor. Tables sat in rows with girls and ladies sitting all around, trimming hats by hand. Trims were never glued on or machine sewn, it was all hand work. All flowers and other shapes were hand made by these ladies.

Trimming was also done as home industry by young mothers and those who chose or could not go out to work. When finished and inspected, hats would be packed for shipping with tissue paper inside a nice hat box.

The ground floor, where you entered the building had the showroom and offices. Buyers made frequent trips to the showroom to see the latest collection and tours of the factory were often conducted.

Groups of buyers were brought to each floor by Mr. Sanders who was the director of the company. I left this industry at age nineteen when I joined Vauxhall Motors as a sewing machinist. The job was sewing car seats, which was boring but paid far more money.

A hat machine made in Berlin by Ernst Bottcher, circa 1890.

VISIBLE STITCH STRAW MACHINE

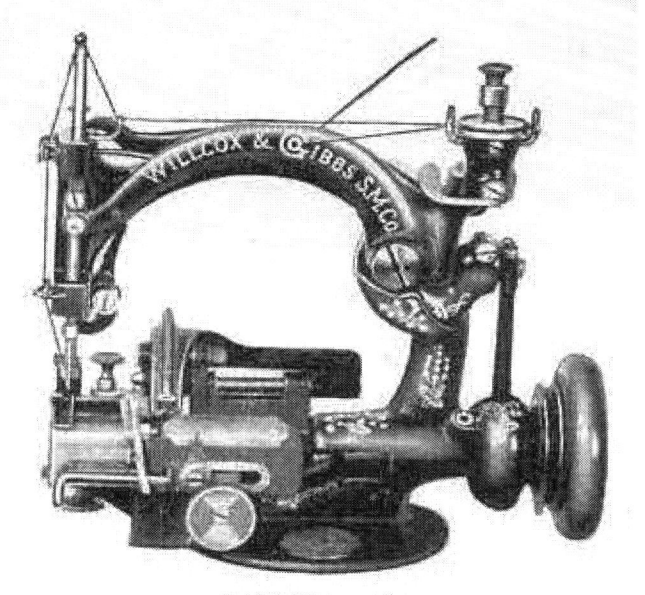

TYPE 200

This was one of the most popular hat machines ever produced. Made by Willcox & Gibbs in New York, it produced a perfect and silent chain stitch. The W&G's model 200 could fly at over 4,000 stiches per minute. A domestic machine today does about 700 spm.

A hat steam press machine circa 1870. They look pretty much the same today. The steam softens the material, like felt, then the press drops over the warm, wet hat and forms it into its shape for around ten minutes. The hat is then left to cool before being trimmed.

Royal Warrant
Geo Bellott,
Hatter & Hosier
Luton

The Heinrich Grossman Dresdenia B hat machine circa 1900 converted to hand but it would have originally sewn on an industrial bench.

A Luton engineer called Edmund Wiseman designed one of the first commercially successful concealed stitch sewing machines in 1878. It was initially manufactured by Willcox & Gibbs but as soon as the patents ran out it was copied by Heinrich Grossman in Dresden and sold by the Janes Brothers of Luton as the H G Lutonia sewing machine. The Lutonia was one of the most successful hat machines of the period between 1900 and 1940. Notice the nice narrow free-arm to allow the hat rims to slide round.

Bulasky hat machine circa 1890. There were many modifications to sewing machines so that they could sew hats, some were modified to sew in the wire hoop on certain hats, some to braid and welt, or add ribbon, some for straw. Many factories made their own modifications.

If an on-site engineer was handy, a machine could be modified for one particular job. This explains why so many varieties of hat machines turn up today. It is important to note if you are buying a hat machine that it does the specific job that you intend or you may end up with a nasty surprise!

This is the amazing Singer model 46-100. It was designed to sew in the sweat bands into felt and straw hats. It always astounds me the minds that could think up, design and make these machines for specialist work.

Walter Wright
Hat Manufacturers
29 Albion Road
Luton

The Singer model 25 came in various guises for hat making. Very rare today, I have only come across one machine in over 40 years. I sold the one below a few years back and miss her. Look at that extraordinary narrow tube-arm!

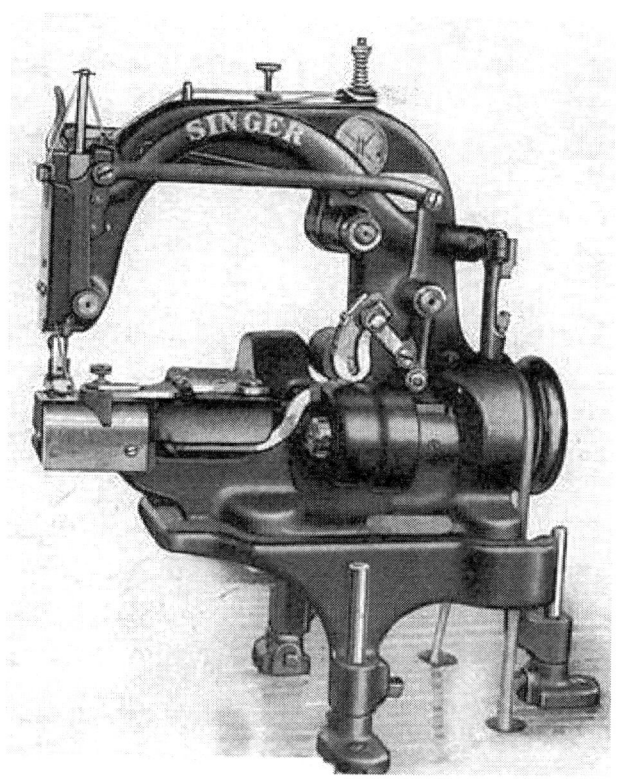

The Singer model 112-1 was a near perfect hat making machine. It had a narrow free arm and made a simple stitch. Tension was adjusted by a top thumbscrew. It was belt driven from steam engines and later electric motors. The machine could manage nearly 3,000 stitches per minute.

This compact industrial model could also do a zig-zag! Notice the great idea of the sliding legs to raise the machine to the perfect height for the operator. Back troubles are still one of the biggest problems for the sewing industry. When this machine was new (around the First World War Era) it would cost the equivalent of a year's wage!

Chapter Seven
Trilby Hat History

Trilby is a funny name for a hat and has an even funnier origin. In 1894 the famous 19th Century author, George du Maurier, published a book with the title Trilby. When it was later made into a stage show, with the character wearing a low short-brimmed hat, with a down turned front, and peeled up back, it instantly caught on.

It was similar to a fedora and made in a variety of materials, from short pile fur, to straw. People referred to it as 'the hat from the play Trilby' and the name stuck. For nearly a century it was one of the most popular hats worn by gangsters and bank managers alike. The lower, snug fitting, stayed on better and allowed easier access to vehicles without having to remove it. In the case of Frank Sinatra, it just looked great.

The Trilby was once seen as a hat of the posh boys and dominated many race meetings as the hat of choice. George du Maurier's granddaughter, Daphne, went on to write such greats as Rebecca and Jamaica Inn.

The World's oldest hat shop-
Lock & Co
6 St James's Street
London
(Established 1676)

**A simple plaited or braided summer or sun hat.
Funny to think that a piece of waste wheat stalk
could be so cleverly crafted into a fine piece of
useful headwear.**

Chapter Eight
Louisa's Story

Her full hilarious story is in my book, Have I Got A Story For You.

Louisa Price was just 20 when the hat making firm she was working in was changed to uniforms for the Second World War. Many of the factories in Luton carried on making hats but for the armed forces instead of civvie-street.

Because Louisa passed a test which she assumed was some sort of IQ test she was moved to a factory set up to manufacture ball bearings for military vehicles, possibly part of the Vauxhall factory.

Here she lined up with all the other girls and was inspected. Louisa had dark eyes, something which was needed for inspecting the finished ball bearings. Dark eyes were supposed to be stronger!

After basic training Louisa had her own room with the sides set up with various containers of liquid to clean and stain the ball bearings before microscopic examination. Her teachers constantly impressed on her the importance of ball bearings in the war effort.

Every machine, every tank, airplane, every car, train and truck ran on ball bearings. They were absolutely vital. If one ball bearing failed so did the machine. If Louisa did not do her job properly Spitfires would fall from the sky and the whole war effort would grind to a halt! She was petrified and made sure she learnt her job perfectly.

After training Louisa started work on her first Monday in her new white coat and long acid proof gloves.

Her first job of the day was to walk around the factory with a wire shopping basket and collect sample bearings from all the machines making them. Then back to her lab and down to business. The ball bearings needed to be de-greased and were dipped in a liquid.

Then they were stained with acid and other chemicals until finally Louisa could get each bearing under the microscope and examine it.

Word soon got around the factory that a new girl had started in the testing lab and two Irishmen turned up with containers for cleaning fluid. A while later two more smiling men turned up for more cleaning fluid, this time with a flask and a saucepan making some poor excuse about the containers. Louisa was polite and chatted to them as she carried on working. This carried on at regular intervals throughout the morning.

By the afternoon Louisa was running low on cleaning fluid and went to her foreman to ask where the supplies were kept. He was astounded. She had enough cleaning fluid for a month not a day! Louisa explained that although she had used some of the fluid most of it was taken by friendly men in all sorts of containers for important work around the plant.

The foreman grunted something unrepeatable. Louisa and her boss then set off to find out what had been happening to her supplies. As they walked around looking for the culprits they heard laughing coming from inside one of the sheds and went to investigate. They found a dozen men drunk as skunks sipping the fluid and singing songs. They all cheered Louisa as she entered and raised their drinking utensils that were an assortment of mugs, cups and jam jars.

No one had told Louisa that the cleaning fluid was pure alcohol! Needless to say she learnt her lesson and never fell for the same old blarney again. After the war she switched back to hat making as if she had never been away.

Great story don't you just love them, real life, real humour in the midst of adversity. Thank you Louisa.

Louisa is currently in her 90's and living in Bexhill-On-Sea. She has the habit of patting my face when I repair her machine as if I have been a good little boy. I just smile, her stories are worth it.

Her full unabridged and hilarious story is in my book Have I Got A Story For You.

Rodney Allison of the North Valley Hat Co in Salem, Oregon, using his Singer 103W3

GODFREY ERMEN'S
500 yds. LUTON GLACE
No. 24 FOR HAND SEWING.
Both are Specially Prepared for the Straw Hat Trade.

Godfrey Ermen,
Thread supplier to the
Luton Hat Trade.

Chapter Nine
Richards & Thirkell (Luton)

One of the more recent successful headwear manufacturing companies in Luton was Richards & Thirkell (Luton) Ltd run by Fredereck Richards, and Claude Thirkell.

In the 1950's Paul Richards, who had done his National Service in Malaysia, (serving in REME attached to the 2/2nd Gurkha Rifles 1951-1953) decided to join his father's business. Richards & Thirkell had an agency dealing in various raw materials for the hat industry.

Paul injected his energy and enthusiasm into the company and looked at ways to improve the business. He studied the hat and millinery supplies throughout the UK, noticing that by the 1950's Luton were mainly concentrating on manufacturing hats for ladies. There was almost nobody in the UK that made headwear for sports. Paul felt that here was a niche market for his business to expand into.

When Paul became managing director of Richards & Thirkell he proceeded to design and produce all types of sports hats and caps, for hunting, fishing, tennis, bowls and golf.

The demand quickly increased, until the company had to sub contract some work out. They soon had agents across Europe, and even one in Punta Arenas, Chile! Paul had a very important shipping agent in Japan, Tsunoda Co. They suppled all the great Japanese stores, Takashimya, Seibu, Mitsakoshi, and others.

The company concentrated on headwear for golf and became the main suppliers to the Royal & Ancient Golf Club of St Andrews, the oldest golf club in the world. At their peak they supplied more than 2,000 clubs in the UK.

The business then expanded into specialised headwear. Paul even designed the Police Marksman cap that is still in use today. Shell, and other oil companies, along with P & O, and many more became regular customers. Richards & Thirkell (Luton) Ltd were one of the modern success stories from Luton.

Paul finally retired to Milton Keynes.

Chapter Ten
The Hat Industry In Portugal

Interestingly it did not matter where hats were being made, they often had some sort of tie with Luton.

In Portugal, a family member that ran one of the few industrial straw hat maker's was Nuno Magalhães.

He told me that the shaping machinery in his business was made by L. Villiers et Cie, Paris. The stitching room composed of several Grossman Dresdensia sewing machines similar to the Willcox & Gibbs 200.

Nuno Magalhães worked with Luton firms like Victor Hyatt and hatters like John Boon, J.G. Page and Burgess Hats (who were at Southend-on-Sea).

Another region of great importance for the hat industry was Firenze – Lastra a Signa, where another cluster of hat producing businesses were well established, mainly: G. Michelanogli & Fgl, and E. Corsani & Fgl. Braga and S. João da Madeira. These were local hot-spots of Portuguese hat making.

Like Luton, and Britain as a whole, the hat trade business declined rapidly in Portugal from the 1960's. Once the invasion of Chinese imports had started in earnest, Portuguese hats became almost redundant, finally collapsing altogether as one factory after another closed.

Interestingly, like Luton and other spots, the hat industry in Portugal is also slowly making a comeback albeit on a small level with specialised hatters hitting individual niche markets.

Chapter Eleven
The Luton Hat Trade Today

The factories that once darkened the skyline have long gone. The whistles and bells, klaxons and horns that people set their watches by have all fallen silent. The countless throng of humanity storming out of the factory gates at closing time are just a distant memory to the few willing to tell their tales.

The crowds that gathered to cheer on Luton Town football team or 'the Hatters' are almost gone too. Their emblem a straw hat and a sheaf of wheat straw. The club that was founded in 1885 has been beset by problems in recent years. The days when their grounds were crammed with workers from the factories are just shadowy memories.

The great news is that there are still a core of hat makers and hat suppliers in Luton. The British Hat

Guild tries to encourage and organise events to promote the ancient trade. The specialised industry keeps part of Luton's rich legacy alive. With the supply of hats, Luton has also maintained a tie with its cultural heritage and a nod to its amazing industrial past.

Who knows, maybe the small enterprises that are flourishing today, (estimated at around 850 people, compared to 100,000 in 1914) may rise again. Luton, the ancient heart of the hat making industry will always hold that historic banner, and can stand proud as a centre of British hat making.

Hats may never regain their supreme standing as a status and class symbol but people will always want to cover their heads. Of course no self-respecting drama department would be seen dead without a storeroom full of period hats. All in all, long live the Luton Hat Industry.

The only museums that I am aware of today as I write, dedicated to hats, are the Luton Hat Factory and one in Stockport, Manchester. The Hat Works Museum of Hatting.

Well that's it folks, as the title tells, a brief history of the Luton Hat Trade with a few interesting anecdotes thrown in. I do hope that you have enjoyed it and it hasn't driven you as mad as a hatter! I tip my cap (no razor blades in sight) and bid you farewell.

Isaac Singer
The First capitalist
No1 New release

Most of us know the name Singer but few are aware of his amazing life story, his rags to riches journey from a little runaway to one of the richest men of his age. The story of Isaac Merritt Singer will blow your mind, his wives and lovers his castles and palaces, all built on the back of one of the greatest inventions of the 19th century. For the first time the most complete story of a forgotten giant is brought to you by Alex Askaroff.

No1 New Release. No1 Bestseller
Amazon certified.

*If this isn't the perfect book it's close to it!
I'm on my third run through already.
Love it, love it, love it.
F. Watson USA*

Elias Howe
The Man Who Changed The World
No1 New Release Amazon Oct 2019.

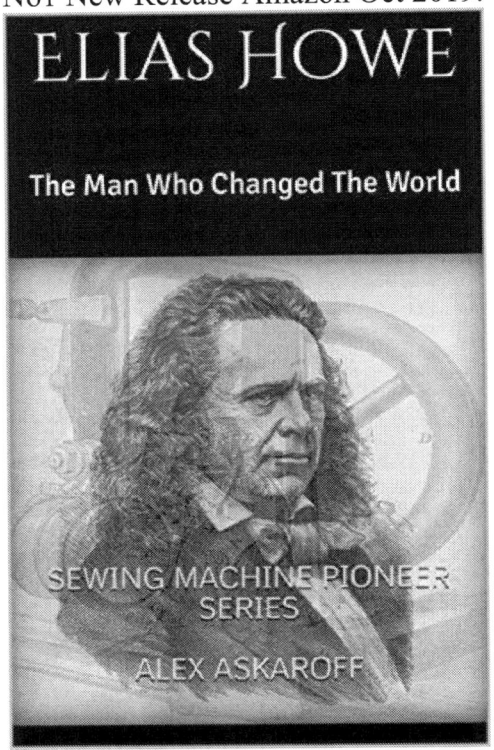

ELIAS HOWE

The Man Who Changed The World

SEWING MACHINE PIONEER SERIES

ALEX ASKAROFF

Anyone who uses a sewing machine today has one person to thank, Elias Howe. He was the young farmer with a weak body who figured it out. Elias's life was short and hard, from the largest court cases in legal history to his adventures in the American Civil War. He carved out a name that will live forever. Elias was 48 when he died. In that short time he really was the man who changed the world.

Printed in Great Britain
by Amazon